LEGITIMACY: FIRST PRINCIPLES AND EFFICACY
IN R2P OPERATIONS

ABSTRACT

LEGITIMACY: FIRST PRINCIPLES AND EFFICACY IN R2P OPERATIONS, by MAJ J. E. LANDRUM, 63 pages.

Legal positivists dominate discussions concerning legitimacy in military operations. From their perspective, the only valid form of legitimacy is an expression of will from sovereign rulers through international organizations. Thus, resolutions from the UN and regional organizations are important prerequisites for military operations. Unfortunately, such a strict focus on procedural expressions of sovereign will leads to irreconcilable paradoxes such as the procedural norms of sovereignty and protection of basic human rights. If states possess a sovereign right of non-interference from external intervention, how then does the international community intervene to protect populations from mass atrocities? Many times the contradiction is not adequately addressed and peacekeepers are deployed to figure it out as they conduct operations. The result is confused operational approaches that lead to decreased efficacy in responsibility to protect operations.

One possible solution to the paradoxes associated with legal positivism is a renewed commitment to the theory of natural law. According to this theory, procedural expressions of sovereign will are absolutely critical to legitimacy, but these expressions must be linked to the antecedent principles of natural law. First principles may serve as a paradox mediator for military decisionmakers as they navigate the complex operating environments associated with humanitarian interventions. In understanding first principles, one must first come to terms with Aristotle's conception of *telos*, which is the Greek word for ends. The ultimate *telos* for international society is to increase the common good. Elections, democracy, sovereignty, and other legal norms are only a means to achieve this good. When they become ends unto themselves, the result is often confusion and a decline in operational efficacy; therefore, planners should constantly refer to teleological first principles when discerning right action in operations.

ACKNOWLEDGMENTS

There is no way this project would have come to fruition without the loving support of my wife, Bevin. Her forbearance during my long hours of study is a great blessing in my life and the source of all my energy. I would also like to thank Dr. Nathan Toronto for his academic advisement. His fortitude in reading through multiple drafts of this document is a great testament to his professionalism and commitment to high academic standards.

TABLE OF CONTENTS

ACRONYMS

AFDL	Alliance for Democratic Forces for the Liberation of Congo
AMIS	African Mission in Sudan
APC	All People's Congress
AU	African Union
CMRRD	Commission for the Management of Strategic Resources, National Reconstruction and Development
DDR	Disarm, Demobilize, and Reintegration
DRC	Democratic Republic of Congo
DPKO	Department of Peacekeeping Operations
ECOMOG	ECOWAS Military Observation Group
ECOWAS	Economic Community of West African States
EO	Executive Outcomes
FARDC	Armed Forces of the Democratic Republic of the Congo
HFCA	Humanitarian Ceasefire Agreement
ICD	Inter-Congolese Dialogue
ICISS	International Convention on Intervention and State Sovereignty
ICOI	International Committee of Inquiry
INPFL	Independent National Patriotic Front of Liberia
MARO	Mass Atrocities Response Operations
MLC	Congo Liberation Movement
NATO	North Atlantic Treaty Organization
NEO	Non-combatant Evacuation
NPRC	National Provisional Ruling Council
NPFL	National Patriotic Front of Liberia
R2P	Responsibility to Protect

RCD	Congolese Rally for Democracy
RPF	Rwanda Patriotic Front
RUF	Revolutionary United Front
SLA	Sierra Leone Army
SLPP	Sierra Leone People's Party
STTT	Short Term Training Team
UN	United Nations
UNAMID	UN/AU Mission in Darfur
UNAMSIL	United Nations Mission in Sierra Leone
UNSC	United Nations Security Council

TABLES

INTRODUCTION

So it is plain that Science must mean the most accurate of all Knowledge; but if so, then the Scientific man must not merely know the deductions from the First Principles but be in possession of truth respecting the First Principles. So that Science must be equivalent to Intuition and Knowledge; it is, so to speak, Knowledge of the most precious objects.

—Aristotle, *Ethics*.

The need for legitimacy in military operations is accepted as an axiomatic truth. However, there is lack of agreement on the source from which legitimacy is derived and what effect it has on the conduct of operations. This is especially true when choosing to use force. Even if the stated purpose is to achieve humanitarian ends, the legitimacy of the use of force is often called into question. Recent events in Libya suggest that the use of force to protect population groups from mass atrocities will continue to be an important mission set for militaries. Given this reality, understanding the nature of legitimacy and how it effects operations is important for the operational artist. Relying too heavily on norms derived from procedural legitimacy may place unnecessary constraints on commanders who hesitate to plan offensive operations to protect non-combatants. Consequently, it is important to understand the relationship between natural law and procedural legitimacy. With a proper understanding of this relationship, commanders and planners will find increased flexibility in the execution of responsibility to protect (R2P) operations.

Literature Review

The principle of R2P was not formally codified until its unanimous inclusion in the 2005 World Outcome Document. Since that time, there have been very few intervention operations executed under the R2P mandate. However, some of the concepts associated with R2P are related to humanitarian interventions in the 1990s; consequently, the literature review will delve into scholarly work examining those phenomenon. It is important to understand that advocates of

1

R2P make a distinction between humanitarian intervention and R2P operations.[1] R2P is an operation focused primarily on the cessation of mass atrocities; whereas, humanitarian interventions have broader implications that range from disaster relief to food delivery. One may consider R2P operations a very specific subset of the broader humanitarian intervention regime. This distinction is important within the debate surrounding R2P operations because many scholars often support R2P operations to prevent mass atrocities while condemning broader operations that fall under humanitarian intervention.

Andrew Hurrell's work provides a solid theoretical discussion concerning the idea of legitimacy. He asserts that legitimacy "refers to a particular kind of rule-following or obedience, distinguishable from purely self-interested behavior on the one hand, and from straightforward imposed or coercive rule on the other."[2] When interveners reference their actions to ideas outside of self-interest, they effectively turn their power into authority. Opponents of intervention use legitimacy as an instrument to challenge the interveners by creating a narrative that the motivations of interveners are mere self-aggrandizement and must be resisted. Interveners seek to develop a narrative that the intervention should be supported as it is being executed for the good of international society.[3] According to Hurrell, "Legitimacy can therefore be seen as a strategic move in a political game and needs to be understood as much a part of the messy world

[1] Thomas G. Weiss, "The Sunset of Humanitarian Intervention? The Responsibility to Protect in a Unipolar Era," *Security Dialouge* 35, no. 2 (2004): 142–144; J.L. Holzgrefe and Robert O. Keohane, *Humanitarian Intervention: Ethical, Legal and Political Dilemmas* (New York: Cambridge University Press, 2003), 18.

[2] Andrew Hurrell, "Legitimacy and the Use of Force: Can the Circle be Squared?," *Review of International Studies* 31(December 2005): 16.

[3] H. Porter Abbot, *The Cambridge Introduction to Narrative* (Cambridge: Cambridge University Press, 2008), 16–22.

of politics as of the idealized world of legal or moral debate."[4]

Hurrell goes on to identify five dimensions of legitimacy: procedural, substantive, specialist, output, and persuasion.[5] Procedural legitimacy emanates from a recognized process that is codified in rules. Known as positivist international law, this kind of legitimacy is achieved through pre-established agreements about approval from constituted authorities such as the United Nations Security Council (UNSC). Substantive legitimacy focuses on principles of justice, democracy, and human rights as possessing higher standing than legal positivists' strict interpretation of procedural approval. Hurrell says substantive appeals "may be viewed in terms of the surreptitious return of natural law ideas or of a philosophically-anchorless, but nevertheless reasonably solid pragmatic consensus."[6] In this monograph, the terms "natural law" and "substantive legitimacy" are used interchangeably. Specialist legitimacy is based on privileged information. For example, the case is made that the international community should act based on special intelligence that cannot be publicly divulged. Output legitimacy is the notion that the effectiveness of a given outcome gives an action its legitimacy. The final dimension of legitimacy is persuasion in which an act is determined as legitimate based on the reasons presented within the context of a persuasive argument.

James Pattison asserts that R2P operations are only legitimate provided they meet two criteria.[7] First, they must be executed to protect basic human rights. Basic human rights are those associated with life and sustenance. They are basic because the inability to live and eat is

----

[4] Hurrell, 16.

[5] Ibid., 18.

[6] Ibid., 21.

[7] James Pattison, *Humanitarian Intervention and the Responsibility to Protect: Who Should Intervene* (New York: Oxford University Press, 2010), 28.

indispensable if other humanitarian rights (e.g., democracy, free speech, and freedom of religion) are to be enjoyed. By focusing strictly on basic human rights, Pattison places a high threshold on the decision to intervene. Second, the consequences of the operation must not be worse than inaction. The second criterion may be considered a "consequentialist" approach to intervention.

Legal positivists dismiss the substantive dimensions of legitimacy as completely unnecessary. Nathaniel Berman suggests that legitimizing appeals to substantive principles such as democracy and human rights are dangerous in that they disrupt the coherence of the international system.[8] For example, the U.S. appealed to substantive principles to protect humanity from weapons of mass destruction in its decision to preemptively invade Iraq. Berman asserts that these appeals unnecessarily destabilize internationalism. Sovereignty and human rights are part of a toolbox from which diplomats can hobble together the necessary mechanisms to achieve internationalist ends. In some cases, this means intervention to protect human rights. In other cases, it means upholding sovereignty and non-intervention.

Corneliu Bjola's work seeks to resolve the conflict between procedural and substantive understandings of legitimacy. According to Bjola, the divide between procedural and substantive legitimacy can be understood as an analytical versus a normative understanding. Those advocates of the procedural dimension of legitimacy are analytical in that they seek to understand "why and how moral or legal norms of legitimacy influence the definition of state interests, foreign policies or the nature of the international order."[9] On the other hand, advocates of the substantive dimension of legitimacy examine "the ethical value of the rules, norms, or principles involved in

---

[8] Nathaniel Berman, "Intervention in a 'Divided World': Axes of Legitimacy, *The European Journal of International Law* 17, no. 4 (2006): 745.

[9] Corneliu Bjola, "Legitimacy and the Use of Force: Bridging the Analytical—Normative Divide," *Review of International Studies* 34 (October 2008): 628.

various definitions of legitimacy."[10] Bjola argues that this divide does not take into account the "normative conditions that facilitate or constrain the definition, contestation, and adjudication of what counts as legitimacy in a particular context."[11] In other words, theorists make a mistake when they separate analytical (legal) and normative (moral) considerations from how states view their interests.

In order to achieve synthesis, Bjola argues that legitimacy must be considered within the context of a fairness and tractability that facilitates deliberative legitimacy. Fairness is the circumstance in which there is mutuality of freely consented restrictions and "a number of persons agree freely, that is, voluntarily and deliberately, to participate and to share proportionally the burdens and benefits of a joint enterprise."[12] This concept provides a moral anchor to the concept of legitimacy. However, fairness must be tractable in that it attracts adherence at a low cost. Tractability seeks to create a win-win situation by acknowledging the human rights concerns of adherents to both points of view. If this approach is adopted, the conditions for deliberative legitimacy are met. According to Bjola, deliberative legitimacy is "the non-coerced commitment of an actor to abide by a decision reached through a process of communicative action."[13] If viewed from this perspective, the epistemological boundary of legitimacy is bridged.

Although much of the literature dealing with legitimacy is abstract in nature, the literature dealing with efficacy is more empirical. Patrick Regan's research on the conditions of successful

---

[10] Ibid., 628.

[11] Ibid., 628.

[12] Ibid., 635.

[13] Ibid., 639.

third-party intervention is useful.[14] He analyzes success in relation to interventions that consist of economic sanctions, military support, or a mix of the two. Regan operationalizes success as the cessation of military hostilities for six months. His conclusion is that mixed interventions on the side of governments are most succesful.

Matthew Krain's work on intervention also examines strategies associated with successful intervention to prevent genocide and politicide.[15] Krain demonstrates that interveners should not remain neutral during an intervention. He argues that "the most effective way for the international community to reduce the severity of an ongoing genocide or politicides is to directly challenge the perpetrator or to aid the target of the brutal policy."[16] Since it essentially identifies offensive operations as important in protecting population groups, this work is especially useful to military planners charged with conducting R2P operations.

An examination of the literature suggests considerable interest in the legitimacy and efficacy of intervention operations. However, there is little study dedicated to how legitimacy is related to the efficacy of R2P operations. Concerns over legitimacy are a significant preoccupation for international diplomats, but it is unclear if these concerns are focused on the proper dimensions of legitimacy. Within international organizations, there is a collective heuristic dominated by legal positivist assumptions about the primacy of procedural instruments, but the paradoxes and dilemmas this heuristic creates impedes timely decision making. These facts are significant considering the amount of killing that can be accomplished in a short amount

---

[14] Patrick M. Regan, "Conditions of Successful Third-Party Intervention in Intrastate Conflicts," *The Journal of Conflict Resolution* 40, no.2 (1996): 343.

[15] Matthew Krain, "International Intervention and the Severity of Genocides and Politicides," *International Studies Quarterly* 49, (September 2005): 363–387.

[16] Ibid., 383.

of time. In the first 100 days of the Rwandan crisis, 800,000 people were killed.[17] The following theoretical discussion demonstrates this argument more clearly.

Theory

According to the Stanford Encyclopedia of Philosophy, "Political legitimacy is a virtue of political institutions and of the decisions—about laws, policies, and candidates for political office—made within them."[18] More specifically, legitimacy is concerned with a basic question: from where do political institutions derive their authority to make and enforce laws or policies? In terms of international relations, this is an important question because states act through international organizations to draft policies they hope will obligate other member states. However, if these organizations are not perceived to possess proper authority, members may not acknowledge an obligation to follow established policies.

Since the nineteenth century, international legal jurisprudence addressed the question of legitimacy through the lens of legal positivism.[19] From this perspective, domestic sovereignty is the possession of sufficient power through which political superiors can physically enforce their will on political inferiors. In such a scenario, the foundation of legitimacy is derived from the principle of might makes right. For example, a tyrannical dictator may establish through decree a legal regime that effectively controls the population through the application of coercive force. In

---

[17] PBS, "Frontline: 100 Days of Slaughter," http://www.pbs.org/wgbh/pages/frontline/shows/evil/etc/slaughter.html (accessed November 12, 2012).

[18] Peter, Fabienne, "Political Legitimacy", *The Stanford Encyclopedia of Philosophy (Summer 2010 Edition)*, ed. Edward N. Zalta , http://plato.stanford.edu/archives/sum2010/entries/legitimacy/.

[19] Stephen Hall, "The Persistent Spectre: Natural Law, International Order and the Limits of Legal Positivism," *European Journal of International Law* 12 no. 2 (2001): 269–307.

this way, legitimacy is derived from physical intimidation. Legitimacy, therefore, is the mere expression of sovereign will. If there is no sovereign, there is no legitimate law. Issues of legitimacy based on *a priori* principles of justice are irrelevant because those principles cannot be empirically verified. In terms of international law, legitimacy is derived from the will of a collection of sovereigns as expressed in observable documents (e.g., treaties and conventions) and customs. International legal positivists claim that sovereign states are not subject to external limitation; however, they may choose to voluntarily submit to international norms established through collective will. Once states choose to submit to the collective will, they are legally bound and unable to reverse the decision.

The irreconcilable dilemmas of legal positivism are readily apparent. If states are really not accountable to external agents, why are they unable to withdraw from the norms of the collective will? Furthermore, the idea of treaties as legally binding expressions of collective will apart from *a priori* principles is misleading. In fact, treaties are merely contractual agreements between sovereign states and can be broken. However, the reality is that states regularly adhere to, though not always, the rights and obligations incurred from treaty agreements. The reason they regularly choose to adhere to treaties is the tacit recognition of the antecedent principle of *pacta sunt servanda*, which is the principle that agreements made should be adhered to. Thus, the obligatory power of treaties comes from the antecedent principle not from an expression of will on paper. Addressing these dilemmas requires an acknowledgement of an *a priori* law—the natural law.[20]

Although many scholars have contributed much to the theory of natural law, Thomas

---

[20] Hedley Bull, "Natural Law and International Relations," *British Journal of International Studies* 5, no. 2 (1979): 171.

Aquinas is noted for being the authoritative voice on the subject.[21] According to Aquinas,

positive law is an indispensable aspect of any legal regime.[22] However, positive law is not

obligatory if it does not operate within the entire system of legal jurisprudence: natural law, *ius*

gentium, and *ius civile*. Natural law is the first principles from which all law is derived, and laws

are only legitimate to the extent that they reflect those principles. *Ius gentium* is a body of

secondary principles in international law, which is based on a deductive interpretation of the first

principles.[23] Finally, *ius civile* is the manifestation of *ius gentium* interpretations of the natural

law in the particulars of legal codes. However, these particulars are only legitimate to the extent

they illuminate natural law. For example, natural law (first principle) dictates, based on a shared

understanding across time and culture, that doing harm to an innocent man is wrong. From this

natural law, *ius gentium* (secondary principle) jurisprudence deduces that murder is wrong.

However, if this law is breached, the jurisprudence of *ius civile* (particular principle) becomes

operative so as to outline the procedures and punishments allocated to the offender.

At its core, natural law is then focused on one overriding *telos* or end, which is to

---

[21] Plato and Aristotle are considered the first scholars to articulate natural law philosophy. As it pertains to international law, Hugo Grotius, a seventeenth century legal scholar, is considered a pioneer in the integration of natural law and the international legal system. In more recent times, Martin Wight and Hedley Bull founded the English School of International Relations, which draws heavily on natural law assumptions in their theories.

[22] Hall, 270.

[23] Hall identifies John Finnis' thirteen general principles of international law as a starting point for understanding *ius gentium*: 1) compulsory acquisition of property rights to be compensated, in respect of *damnum emergens* (actual losses) if not of *lucrum cessans* (loss of expected profits); 2) no liability for unintentional injury, without fault; 3) no criminal liability without *mens rea*; 4) estoppels; 5) no judicial aid to one who pleads his own wrong; 6) no aid to abuse of rights; 7) fraud unravels everything; 8) profits received without justification and at the expense of another must be resored; 9) *pacta sunt servanda*; 10) relative freedom to change existing patterns of legal relationships by agreement; 11) the weak to be protected against their weakness; 12) disputes not to be resolved without giving both sides an opportunity to be heard; 13) no one to be allowed to judge his own cause.

increase the common good. Drawing on Aristotelian philosophy, Alasdair MacIntyre says that good "is the state of being well and doing well in being well, of a man being well-favored himself and in relation to the divine."[24] Obtaining the common good is the driving force behind right action. In Aristotle's day, the good life was only obtained in the context of humans living virtuously within the society of a city-state. However, the new reality is that humans increasingly cooperate within the context of an international society, and there is an embryonic notion that the common good lies in protecting the dignity of individual human beings.[25] Therefore, when executing R2P operations, all decisions for right action must illuminate those first principles that best facilitate the advancement of the common good in international society.

Unfortunately, the hegemony of the legal positivist heuristic renders this system ineffective. Without the mediating effect of the substantive principles of natural law, the dictates emanating from international organizations suffer from confusion and contradiction. In situations where mass atrocities are occurring, diplomats in international organizations feel compelled to respond to the antecedent principles of the common good in mass atrocities; however, they are often constrained by a legal positivist heuristic that places the secondary principle of sovereignty on equal footing with first principles associated with human security. This slows down or inhibits initial responses. Once a response does occur, military leaders, indoctrinated by a legal positivist heuristic, try to determine courses of action that satisfy all the tenants of procedural norms. In many cases, commanders choose the pacific settlement of disputes as outlined in Chapter VI of the UN Charter over the use of force to protect individuals as outlined in Chapter VII of the UN

---

[24] Alasdair MacIntyre, *After Virtue*, 3rd ed. (Notre Dame: Notre Dame University Press, 2008), 148.

[25] Daniel Philpott, *Revolutions in Sovereignty* (Princeton: Princeton University Press, 2001), Kindle e-reader, location 344–415.

Charter. The hypothesis of this monograph is that the dominance of a legal positivist heuristic decreases the efficacy of R2P operations.

This monograph is divided into five sections. The first section is the introduction comprised of the literature review, critical definitions, and methodology. The second section examines competing notions of sovereignty. The third section is a brief examination of how the principle of R2P developed since the end of the Cold War. The point of this examination is to provide a theoretical framework for understanding how different actors view the forms of legitimacy for implementing R2P. Section four is an examination of the case studies. In the final section, the findings of the case study analyses are presented.

Definitions and Methodology

In discussing R2P, it is important to understand there is a wide range of opinions as to what exactly constitutes an R2P operation. The International Committee on Intervention and State Sovereignty (ICISS) committee identified three types of R2P operations: prevent, react, and rebuild.[26] Prevent suggests operations that seek to build functional institutions in an effort to thwart mass atrocities before they start. React is a "forcible military action by an external agent in the relevant political community with the predominant purpose of preventing, reducing, or halting an ongoing or impending grievous suffering or loss of life."[27] Finally, the rebuild type of R2P operation is focused on assisting the target nation to rebuild after humanitarian intervention (react) operations; the need for the rebuild operation assumes that military operations are fairly

---

[26] Gareth Evans and Mohamed Sahnoun, *Report of the International Convention on Intervention and Sovereignty*, http://responsibilitytoprotect.org/ICISS%20Report.pdf (accessed, January 12, 2013).

[27] James Pattison, *Humanitarian Intervention and the Responsibility to Protect: Who Should Intervene* (New York: Oxford University Press, 2010), 28.

destructive of the target state's infrastructure. This monograph focuses on the react dimension of R2P, which is essentially a sub-component of the broader R2P concept.

The literature suggests there are two sources of procedural legitimacy for R2P operations: UNSC and regional organization approval.[28] From the very beginning, diplomats have asserted that the UNSC is the highest source of legitimacy for R2P operations. According to the 2001 ICISS report, "There is no better or more appropriate body than the United Nations Security Council to authorize military intervention for human protection purposes."[29] Most diplomats have no disagreement with this statement. However, the ICISS report also suggests there are other sources of legitimacy if the UNSC is politically incapable of action.

The ICISS document proposes that the approval of regional organizations provides adequate legitimacy for R2P operations. According to the report, "If the Security Council rejects a proposal or fails to deal with it in a reasonable time, alternative options are within the area of jurisdiction by regional or sub-regional organizations under Chapter VIII of the Charter, subject to their seeking subsequent authorization from the Security Council."[30] In the case studies of this monograph, procedurally legitimate interventions are those in which approval for intervention was justified through the approval of either the UNSC or a regional organization.

Substantive legitimacy is defined as an R2P operation that is legitimized on the basis of appeals to the requirements of moral principles to protect basic human rights.[31] Separating substantive legitimacy from procedural legitimacy is problematic, for procedural documents such

---

[28] Ibid., 34.

[29] Alex J. Bellamy, *Responsibility to Protect* (Cambridge: Polity Press, 2009), 57.

[30] Ibid., 57.

[31] Pattison, 28.

as UNSC resolutions assume a substantive principle.[32] However, state(s) may decide to intervene without the *imprimatur* of a UNSC resolution, which suggests that substantive principles may be examined separately.

These observations allow for an examination of legitimacy within four possible categories: maximum, high, low and minimal. Maximum legitimacy occurs when the legitimizing agents are comprised of a UNSC resolution, regional organization approval, and appeals to substantive principles. High legitimacy occurs when the legitimizing agents are merely a UNSC resolution and appeals to substantive principles. Low legitimacy occurs when there is no UNSC approval; however, a regional organization approves intervention on the basis of an appeal to substantive principles. Finally, minimum legitimacy occurs when a state or group of states intervene in the absence of approval from either the UNSC or a regional organization.

Table 1 provides a visualization of this definitional approach.

Table 1: Levels of Legitimacy

	UN	REGIONAL	SUBSTANTIVE
Maximum	X	X	X
High	X		X
Low		X	X
Minimum			X

Source: Created by author

---

[32] As stated previously, legal positivists would deny the assumption of substantive principles in procedural legitimacy; however, this monograph assumes the existence, whether acknowledged or denied, of the antecedent principles of international law.

Efficacy in R2P operations is focused on preventing mass atrocities against population groups. According to Sarah Sewall and John Kardos, "A Mass Atrocity Response Operation (MARO) describes a contingency operation to halt the widespread and systematic use of violence by state or non-state armed groups against non-combatants."[33] The handbook goes on to describe the end state conditions for a MARO: "Widespread mass atrocity is stopped or prevented and is unlikely to occur in the future."[34] Based on these criteria, efficacy in R2P operations is defined as cessation in the systematic use of violence against non-combatants.

THE HISTORY OF SOVEREIGNTY: FICTIONS, IDEAS, AND REVOLUTIONS

According to the commonly accepted understanding of sovereignty, states possess it when they have a definable territory and the ability to control populations. States recognized as existing under such conditions are acknowledged in the broader international system and subsequently receive all the rights and privileges of a sovereign. The most important of these rights is the right of non-intervention from external actors. These facts are normative and regulate diplomacy in the international political system.

Stephen Krasner challenges the idea that such a norm of sovereignty and non-intervention actually exists. On the contrary, the international system is maintained by rulers who make decisions to maximum utility. Because a coherent international system reduces transaction costs thereby making future agreements more likely, rulers often recognize the sovereignty of other

---

[33] Sarah Sewell, Dwight Raymond, and Sally Chin, *Mass Atrocities Response Operations: A Military Planner's Handbook* (Boston: Harvard University Press, 2010), 55.

[34] Ibid., 57.

states.[35] However, if the utility of violating sovereignty is greater than the utility of honoring sovereignty, states routinely choose to violate. Thus, the very notion of an international norm of sovereignty is an organized hypocrisy to disguise the base desire of rulers to maintain power.[36]

When it comes to human rights, Krasner argues that rulers do not choose to uphold human rights based on an international norm. Instead, rulers often feel pressured by domestic audiences to pursue such arrangements. Furthermore, rulers often have an interest in securing an international script of human rights for their people in the future. In this way, human rights are not related to some *a priori* notion in natural law; it is the result of the rational choice of various rulers. Krasner's argument is persuasive, but he does not fully account for the power of ideas and societies in international relations. He does not answer the question about why domestic audiences and rulers even desire a human rights regime in the first place. The answer to this question may only be answered through a teleological approach that recognizes a common good outside of interests.[37]

Daniel Philpott uses the work of Hedley Bull and Adam Watson to define international society as "a group of states (or, more generally, a group of independent political communities) which have established by dialogue and consent to common rules and institutions for the conduct

---

[35] In regime theory, a reduction in transaction costs means that various international regimes establish understood procedural rules in which to cooperate. Because these rules are agreed upon in advance, it facilitates negotiations and increases the likelihood of future agreements being honored. For example, the International Civil Aviation Organization (ICAO) is a regime with established rules about air space, air traffic controllers, and transportation of hazardous materials that reduce the cost of cooperation in international aviation.

[36] Stephen Krasner, *Sovereignty: Organized Hypocrisy* (Princeton: Princeton University Press, 1999), Kindel e-reader, locaton 25.

[37] Ibid., Kindle e-reader, location 1383.

of their relations, and recognize their common interest in maintaining these arrangements."[38] These rules and institutions are formed on the basis of ideas that are created by opinion leaders and subsequently spread to international society.

Within these international societies, opinion leaders advocated ideas about sovereignty that were eventually adopted.[39] When these ideas were adopted, a revolution in sovereignty occurred. In terms of the modern state system, there were two significant revolutions in sovereignty. The first revolution occurred in Western Europe when the various polities rejected attempts at centralized control emanating from the Holy Roman Empire with the 1648 Peace of Westphalia. This revolution established the modern state system and the implicit principle of non-intervention among states. The second revolution occurred at the end of World War Two when the modern state system was extended to other parts of the world. Colonial possessions rejected outside rule and demanded a right to self-determination. Since the end of the Cold War, international society is once again redefining the limits of sovereignty, and this is challenging strongly held assumptions about the legitimacy of external intervention in the internal affairs of states. Therefore, Krasner is right in that sovereignty is negotiable, and Phipott is right in that this negotiation occurs within the context of an international society seeking the common good.

R2P AS REVOLUTION: CONFLICTING NOTIONS OF LEGITIMACY

After the Cold War, interstate war declined as the overriding concern of international society. According to Gareth Evans, "The quintessential peace and security problem became not interstate war, but civil war, and internal violence perpetrated on a massive scale. With the

---

[38] Daniel Philpott, *Revolutions in Sovereignty: How Ideas Shaped Modern International Relations* (Princeton: Princeton University Press, 2001), Kindle e-reader, location 380.

[39] Philpott, Kindle e-reader, location 1090.

breakup of various cold war state structures, most obviously in Yugoslavia, and the removal of superpower constraints, conscience-shocking situations repeatedly arose."[40] In places like Somalia, Rwanda, and Srebrenica, the international community witnessed violations of basic human rights on a massive scale, and they were unable to do anything to effectively stop the atrocities. In many cases, international society invoked non-intervention for the reason behind inaction.

As a result, Koffi Annan addressed the General Assembly in 1999 and challenged member states to reevaluate their understanding of sovereignty and humanitarian intervention.[41] In this speech, Annan made it clear that the inability of the UN to act in the face of these mass atrocities would ultimately discredit the institution with the people of the world. From Annan's point of view, there is no way that an organization explicitly devoted to the idea of peace and security could stand aside while innocent civilians suffered under the hands of tyranny and violence. Annan was redefining the discussion on the legitimacy of sovereignty when basic human rights were being violated.

Annan's call to address concerns about sovereignty and humanitarian intervention was answered in 2000. Sponsored by the Canadian government, the ICISS was established to research possible resolutions of the dilemma between sovereignty and human rights. Although endorsed by Koffi Annan, ICISS was not an official UN endeavor. The committee was chaired by diplomats Gareth Evans (Australia) and Mohammed Sahnoun (Algeria); the subordinate commissioners were from various locations around the world. Thus, the perspectives outlined in

---

[40] Gareth Evans, "The Responsibility to Protect: From an Idea to an International Norm," in *Responsibility to Protect: The Global Moral Compact for the 21st Century*, ed. Richard H. Cooper and Juliette Voinov Kohler (New York: Palgrave-Macmillan, 2009), 17.

[41] Koffi Annan, *1999 Speech to the General Assembly*, Secretary-General address to the UN General Assembly, New York, NY, September 20, 1999.

the ICISS document are broadly representative of the thinking on sovereignty and human rights. After ten conferences, the legitimacy of humanitarian intervention was debated, and new ways of resolving the dilemma were explored.

Based on the output from these conferences, Francis Cheng and Roberta Cohen first formulated the idea of Responsibility to Protect (R2P).[42] To resolve the dilemma between the concepts, Cheng and Cohen suggested the issue be viewed from the perspective of the victims. From this perspective, states have a responsibility to protect citizens from mass atrocities. If they are unwilling or unable to meet this responsibility, international society has a responsibility to intervene on behalf of the oppressed. This was the guiding principle in the final ICISS report. Gareth Evans incorporated these ideas in an academic paper in which he tried to change the discourse on the topic.

Advocates of R2P view the ICISS report as a foundational document. It sought to address all the concerns about the conflict between human rights and sovereignty. In the first section of the document, there is a clear procedural legitimizing criterion for intervention. Legitimate R2P intervention was limited to "large scale loss of life" and "large scale 'ethnic cleansing', actual or apprehended, whether carried out by killing, forced expulsion, acts of terror or rape."[43] In making the criteria for R2P so high, the authors of the ICISS document hoped to address the concerns of critics concerned about the arbitrary evocation of the principle. Furthermore, the document draws on just war theory citing right intention, last resort, proportional means, and reasonable prospect of success as guiding principles.

---

[42]Bellamy, 35–66.

[43] Gareth Evans and Mohamed Sahnoun, *Report of the International Convention on Intervention and Sovereignty*, http://responsibilitytoprotect.org/ICISS%20Report.pdf (accessed, January 12, 2013).

The ICISS document then identifies the UNSC as the highest and most desired level of authority. However, the document tried to overcome some of the political obstacles to intervention with a provision that P5 members "should agree not to apply their veto power, in matters where their vital state interests are not involved, to obstruct the passage of resolutions authorizing military intervention for human protection purposes for which there is otherwise majority support."[44] If for political reasons the UNSC was unable to approve action, the ICISS document clearly identified other sources of procedural legitimacy. For example, the UN General Assembly and regional organizations could provide procedural legitimacy to R2P interventions.

Opposition to the document came from every point of view. The United States objected to any restrictions being placed on the use of force as it deemed necessary. Other P5 members balked at the suggestion of giving up their veto power in any circumstance. Representing the non-aligned movement, India's rejection reflected Nathaniel Bergman's argument that there were already procedural mechanisms in place to deal with humanitarian crises when necessary. Ironically, the African states, arguably the most affected from past imperialism, were supportive of the idea of the R2P norm; however, this is not surprising since the African Union made humanitarian intervention permissible in their 2000 Constitutive Act. In order to address these concerns, Kofi Annan put R2P on the agenda of his 2004 High Level Panel on Threats.[45]

In preparation for the 2005 World Outcome Summit, Kofi Annan commissioned the 2004 High Level Panel (HLP) on Threats, and he ensured Gareth Evans was on the panel. Evans worked hard to ensure the fundamentals of the ICISS document remained intact. However, modifications were unavoidable. The most substantial change to the ICISS document was the

_____

[44] Ibid.

[45] Bellamy, 55–60.

issue of the P5 veto. Instead of limiting veto powers, the HLP called for indicative voting, which required vetoes to be publicly declared and explained. The hope was that the idea of explaining an anti-humanitarian veto would shame members into compliance. The HLP also removed language that condoned action outside of the UNSC. With these modifications, the concerns were addressed and the R2P terminology was included in the 2005 World Outcome Document, which was approved with a unanimous UN vote in September.[46]

CASE STUDIES

The unit of observation is a cross-case analysis of five R2P operations: Darfur, Democratic Republic of Congo (DRC), Liberia, Sierra Leone, and Libya. Darfur, DRC, and Liberia provide the primary case studies of interest in that each case presents an example in which a procedurally legitimate R2P operation was executed. Darfur was a maximum level intervention. The DRC is an example of high level intervention, and Liberia is a low level intervention. Sierra Leone is a case study of minimal level intervention in that the intervener appealed only to substantive principles of protection of basic human rights as the legitimizing agent. In order to avoid over determinacy, the research design follows King, Keohane, and Verba's guideline to include a negative case study to introduce variance on the dependent variable.[47] To this end, the monograph will examine the case of Libya as an example where maximum legitimacy led to an effective R2P operation.

There are weaknesses in these case selections. The most glaring being the fact that Africa is an extremely heterogeneous continent. According to King, Keohane, and Verba, "The

---

[46] Ibid., 55–60.

[47] Gary King, Robert O. Keohane, and Sidney Verba, *Designing Social Inquiry: Scientific Inference in Qualitative Research* (Princeton: Princeton University Press, 1994), Kindle e-reader, location 2199–2870.

notion of unit homogeneity (or the less demanding assumption of constant causal effects) lies at the base of all scientific research."[48] In order to ensure for constant causal effects, the selected case studies are all from Africa and exclude interventions in other parts of the world. Including countries outside Africa would cause measurement problems since efficacy is caused by other factors such as the level of economic and institutional development.

Darfur: Maximum Level Intervention

In 1989, President Omar Hassan Ahmad al Bashir came to office in a military coup that was backed by the Muslim Brotherhood. He was the head of the National Liberation Front, which was Arab dominated and aimed to instill political Islam into Sudanese politics. In ruling from Khartoum, Bashir implemented policies favoring Arab herders at the expense of African agriculturalists. Because of this favoritism, the UN International Commission of Inquiry (ICI) report states that tribes coalesced around African and Arab identities despite a common language and religion. [49]

In the winter of 2003, the African Sudanese Liberation Army (SLA) and the Justice and Equality Movement (JEM) launched a rebellion against the Sudanese government.[50] The government responded with devastating attacks with their main force units. However, it was the mobilization of the *Janjaweed* militia units that caused the most devastation. The *Janjaweed* militias practiced systematic ethnic cleansing of opposition groups. Tactics included the burning of villages, murder, and rape. By September of 2004, the Sudanese main forces and *Janjaweed*

---

[48] Ibid., Kindle e-reader, location 1803.

[49] International Commission of Inquiry, *Report of the International Commission of Inquiry on Darfur to the United Nations Secretary General* (New York, 2004), 22.

[50] Aidan Hehir, *Humanitarian Intervention After Kosovo: Iraq, Darfur and the Record of Global Civil Society* (New York: Palgrave Macmillan, 2008), 65–70.

militia displaced 1.2 million people. Of those 1.2 million displaced persons, approximately 200,000 migrated into neighboring Chad thereby creating a refugee crisis.[51]

Guided by the slogan "African Solutions to African Problems," the AU was the first organization to commit to facilitating a settlement in the Sudanese conflict.[52] In April of 2004, AU special representative to Darfur, Baba Gana Kingie, met with representative from all parties in N'Djamena, Chad to discuss peace terms. The result was the Humanitarian Ceasefire Agreement (HFCA). According to the HFCA, all conflicting parties agreed to a ceasefire, the AU was authorized a military presence in Darfur to facilitate the delivery of humanitarian aid, and the government of Sudan agreed to disarm the *Janjaweed* militia groups. Known as the African Union Mission in Sudan (AMIS), the peacekeepers deployed to Darfur in May 2004.

With only 80 observers and 300 security personnel, there was little that AMIS could accomplish in its early deployment. The evidence suggests that Bashir and the government of Sudan were manipulating procedural legitimacy to facilitate their destructive campaign in Darfur. While they ostensibly agreed to the HFCA provisions, the government of Sudan ignored the provisions of the HFCA and civilian deaths continued unabated. Secretary General Koffi Annan met with Bashir in July 2004 to persuade him to honor the HFCA. The result was a Joint Communiqué in which the government of Sudan once again agreed to disarm the *Janjaweed*, allow the deployment of human rights monitors, and ensure that those responsible for human rights violations were brought to justice. The Joint Communiqué did little to change the reality in Darfur. In response, the UNSC passed resolution 1556 in July 2004 threatening sanctions against

---

[51] Ibid., 66.

[52] Cristina Badescu and Linnea Bergholm, "The African Union," in *The International Politics of Mass Atrocities: The Case of Darfur* ed. David R. Black and Paul D. Williams (New York: Routledge Publishers, 2010), 101–103.

the government of Sudan.

At this point, the international community had utilized three procedural instruments to thwart the mass atrocities occurring in Darfur: the HFCA, the Joint Communiqué, and UNSC resolution 1556. In keeping with their established diplomatic practice, the government of Sudan agreed to these procedural restraints while continuing their campaign of killing. By the end of July 2004, the operations of the Sudanese Army and *Janjaweed* militias killed between 30,000-50,000 civilians.[53]

Although plagued with internal debate concerning the sovereignty of Sudan, the Peace and Security Council of the AU reacted to these failures by agreeing in 2005 to increase the number of personnel on the ground to more than 2,000 personnel. According to Badescu and Bergholm, the increased troop levels were marginally effective in improving security in Darfur:

> The increase in numbers did contribute positively to the security situation. During 2005, the IDPs were congregating near the AMIS bases and the UN World Food Program started parking its vehicles at AMIS sites. AMIS escorted humanitarian convoys and helped victims of attacks get to hospitals. Nevertheless, the enhanced force levels were not enough for AMIS to make a significant contribution toward civilian protection.[54]

Part of the problem contributing to AMIS failure in protecting civilians was a lack of clarity on mandate. There were politicians within the Peace and Security Council calling for a proactive approach for protecting the population. Remembering his country's ordeal with mass atrocities in 1993, Rwandan president Paul Kagame declared that his forces would not "stand by and watch innocent civilians being hacked to death like the case was here in 1994. Our forces will intervene

---

[53] Samuel Totten, "Saving Lives in Darfur, 2003-2006?" in *The World and Darfur: International Response to Crimes Against Humanity in Western Sudan,* ed. Amanda F. Gryzyb (Kingston: McGill-Queen's University Press, 2009), 190.

[54] Bedescu and Bergohm, 104.

and use force to protect civilians."[55] However, Sudanese diplomats within the AU purposefully

worked to make the AMIS mandate weak and ambiguous. For example, Sudan ensured AMIS

was only able to protect civilians within their immediate vicinity; the government of Sudan was

responsible for protecting the civilian population in general. According to a Human Security

Gateway report, Sudanese manipulation of the AU was a key fact in the inability of AMIS to

make progress in Darfur:

> Efforts of the AU to deploy an effective military force into Darfur were also
> crippled by Sudan's maneuvering within the AU institutions especially the Peace
> and Security Council. Despite its cardinal role in the security and humanitarian
> crisis in Darfur and the African sub-region, GoS served as a full-fledged member
> in the first AU Peace and Security Council (2003-2006).[56]

Throughout the entire Darfur crises, the Sudanese government displayed an uncanny ability to

outmaneuver regional and international diplomats.

Despite the fact that the AU eventually authorized the deployment of 7,000 personnel,

AMIS did not have the resources it needed to protect victimized population groups. A major

factor preventing greater support for AMIS was a procedural road block in the form of an

inability to declare that genocide was occurring in Darfur. In September 2004, the US convinced

the Security Council to pass UNSC resolution 1564, which initiated the International Commission

of Inquiry on Darfur (COI) to determine whether the government of Sudan was engaged in

genocidal activities. After a three month investigation, the COI reported back in January 2005

that the government of Sudan was not engaged in genocide. The COI reasoned that the Bashir

regime did not demonstrate intent to commit genocide:

> The crucial element of genocidal intent appears to be missing, at least as far as

---

[55] Ibid., 105.

[56] Abdelbagi A. M. Jibril, *Past and Future of UNAMID: Tragic Failure or Glorious Success?* (Geneva: Darfur Relief and Documentation Center, 2010), 14.

the central government authorities are concerned. Generally speaking the policy of attacking, killing and forcibly displacing members of some tribes does not evince a specific intent to annihilate, in whole or in part, a group distinguished on racial, ethnic, national, or religious grounds. Rather, it would seem that those who planned and organized attacks on villages pursued the intent to drive the victims from their homes, primarily for purposes of counter-insurgency warfare. The Commission does recognize that in some instances individuals, including Government officials, may commit acts with genocidal intent. Whether this was the case in Darfur, however, is a determination that only a competent court can make on a case by case basis.[57]

However, the COI did conclude that serious humanitarian crimes were committed and that they were "no less serious and heinous than genocide."[58] This finding was based on a strict interpretation of "intent" as outlined in the 1948 UN Declaration on the Prevention and Punishment of the Crime of Genocide. According to this definition, there must be "intent to destroy, in whole or in part, a national, ethnic, racial or religious group."[59] If the commission had determined genocide was being perpetrated, the international community would have been obliged to increase its support to AMIS.[60]

Prior to the COI report, the US government unilaterally determined that the Sudanese government was engaged in genocidal activities. Citing appeals to substantive legitimacy, the US congress passed a resolution encouraging the Bush administration to "seriously consider multilateral or even unilateral intervention to stop genocide in Darfur, Sudan, should the United Nations Security Council fail to act; and to impose targeted sanctions, including visa bans and the freezing of assets of the Sudanese National Congress and affiliated business and individuals

---

[57] International Commission of Inquiry, *Report of the International Commission of Inquiry on Darfur to the United Nations Secretary General* (New York, 2004).

[58] Ibid.

[59] Ibid.

[60] Totten, 192.

directly responsible for atrocities."[61] However, the Bush administration was too preoccupied with the wars in Iraq and Afghanistan to act on such resolutions. Moreover, the Bashir regime was giving ostensible support to US counterterrorism efforts in Africa. To be sure, the US funneled large amounts of humanitarian support to Darfur, but the US never made any serious attempts to provide hard military assistance, apart from logistical and transportation support, to AMIS forces on the ground.

By the end of 2006, there were more than 6,000 AMIS troops in Sudan. However, they lacked the training, resources, and mandate to protect the population, and they were unable to stop the Sudanese killing of civilians. Despite the lack of procedural legitimacy in the form of a UN declaration of genocide, diplomats in the international community continued to appeal substantive principles as a basis for a Chapter VII UN mission in Darfur. However, the Sudanese government made clear that a UN force would be considered hostile. Despite these threats, UNSC resolution 1706 was passed in August 2006 inviting the government of Sudan to consent to the deployment of UN forces. Through negotiations led by Secretary General Annan, the Bashir regime finally agreed to a compromise plan that created a hybrid force of the United Nations and the African Union: United Nations-African Union Mission in Darfur (UNAMID). In keeping the AU part of the mission, Khartoum was able to maintain an ability to manipulate the conduct of UNAMID through their membership in the AU. UNSC resolution authorized the deployment of UNAMID in 2007.

UNAMID's primary mandate was to protect civilians in Darfur; however, the government of Sudan used its position as a member of the AU to impose restrictions and limitations that rendered UNAMID ineffective. For example, most of the troop contributors to

---

[61] Ibid., 197.

26

UNAMID came from countries friendly to the government of Sudan; therefore, the perception among many Darfurians was that UNAMID was pro-Khartoum. Furthermore, the Bashir regime forbade Western and Latin American soldiers from being part of the organization. These restrictions resulted in states being reluctant to deploy "necessary technical expertise and crucial equipment including means of transport, communication, logistics and combat helicopter which are equipment necessary for an effective military operation."[62]

According to Abdelbagi Jibril, the popular resentment with ineffective protection turned to attacks and protests against UNAMID forces:

> Increase in the number and frequency of incidents of aggression against UNAMID soldiers and personnel including, killings, armed attacks and stone throwing indicate that UNAMID is disdained, resented and mistrusted by all the stakeholders in Darfur including the IDPs and the war affected civilian populations as well as Darfur insurgent groups and the GoS whose solders had launched the first ever armed attack against UNAMID in January 2008.[63]

However, the plight of the Darfurian civilians in the first year of UNAMID's operation is the most condemning fact. During that year, Human Security Gateway, a human rights NGO in Canada, claims that "militia attacks, violence, tribal fighting, and military operations rendered 317,000 people as internally displaced, often for the second or third time since the conflict in Darfur started in early 2003."[64] By any objective standard, the UNAMID experiment was ineffective.

---

[62] Abdelbagi A. M. Jibril, *Past and Future of UNAMID: Tragic Failure or Glorious Success?* (Geneva: Darfur Relief and Documentation Center, 2010), 14.

[63] Jibril, 14.

[64] Ibid., 7.

Democratic Republic of the Congo: High Level Intervention

The United Nations Organization Mission in the Democratic Republic of Congo (MONUC) provides an example of a high level intervention. The mission was authorized under UNSC resolution 1291 in February 2000 and was to consist of 5,537 peacekeeping personnel with a Chapter VII mandate to "protect civilians under imminent threat of physical violence."[65] However, the deployment of MONUC was extremely slow. By June 2001, MONUC only had 2,366 military personnel on the ground. Because of the slow deployment, MONUC failed to protect the population resulting in UNSC resolution 1565, which was drafted in October 2004 making civilian protection a primary objective. To accomplish this expanded mandate, the UNSC authorized the deployment of an additional 5,900 troops. The deployment of MONUC was executed according to a three phased plan: deployment of a UN liaison team, deployment of military observers, and deployment of peacekeeping force.

In 1993, the civil war in Rwanda between the Hutu dominated government of Rwanda and the Tutsi led Rwandan Patriotic Front (RPF) was raging. The conflict became regional as Congolese and Ugandan Tutsis crossed the border to join their brethren in battle. When Rwandan President Juvenal Habyarimana was killed, radicals in the Hutu government responded with a genocide in which 800,000 Tutsis were exterminated.[66] The same event played out between the Bayarwandan Hutu and Tutsis in the DRC's eastern Kivu provinces; however, the DRC's military forces were able to quell the violence before it got too far out of control.[67] When the Rwanda

---

[65] United Nations, *MONUC: United Nations Mission in the Democratic Republic of the Congo*, http://www.un.org/en/peacekeeping/missions/monuc/mandate.shtml (accessed November 12, 2012).

[66] Severine Autesserre, *The Trouble with the Congo: Local Violence and the Failure of Peacebuilding* (Cambridge: Cambridge University Press, 2010), 131–142.

[67] Hutu and Tutsis are not native to the DRC. However, during their colonial rule, the

Patriotic Front (RPF) toppled the Hutu dominated government in Rwanda in 1994, more than 2 million Hutu refugees crossed the border into the DRC in fear of reprisals for the mass killings.[68] Among this number were former members of the Rwandan Army who were complicit in the genocide.

Once in the DRC, the Hutus attacked Banyarwandan Tutsis and launched raids into Rwanda and Uganda. Fed up with the DRC's inability to control its eastern provinces, Rwanda, Uganda, and Burundi backed the creation of the Alliance for Democratic Forces for the Liberation of Congo (AFDL). This was the start of the First Congo War that lasted from September 1996-May 1997. At the end of the conflict, Mobutu, the country's dictator, was ousted, and the leader of the AFDL, Laurent Desire Kabila, assumed control of the country. He promptly changed the name of the country from Zaire to the Democratic Republic of the Congo.

Kabila proved unwilling to stop the cross border raids into Rwanda, and he continued to persecute the Banyarwandans. When he demanded the removal of Rwandan military advisers left over from the First Congo War, Kabila's former allies turned against him. Rwanda, Uganda, and Burundi sponsored a new rebel group known as the Congolese Rally for Democracy (RCD). This was the start of the Second Congo War that lasted from August 1998-July 1999. Because of a falling out between the governments of Uganda and Rwanda, the RCD split into two sub-factions: RCD-Goma (Rwanda) and RCD-Kisangani (Uganda). In this chaos, a third rebel group emerged known as the Congo Liberation Movement (MLC), which was comprised mostly of former Mobutists seeking to regain power. However, unlike Mobutu in the previous war, Kabila had the backing of other countries in the region: Angola, Namibia, Chad, and Sudan. With this support,

---

Belgians encouraged the migration of Hutus and Tutsis from Rwanda as labor for plantation work. Thus, Banyarwanda (people from Rwanda) Hutus and Tutsis make up a large ethnic minority in the eastern Kivu region of the DRC.

[68] Autessere, 47.

he was able to defend part of the DRC. By July 1999, the opposing forces had essentially reached a stalemate with Kabila forces holding ground in the west and the various rebel groups in conjunction with neighboring armies (Uganda, Rwanda, Angola, Namibia, and Zimbabwe) splitting terrain in the east. The war was truly a regional conflict, and the international community was keen to mediate a cessation to the hostilities. The result of these negotiations was the drafting of three procedural instruments: the Lusaka Agreement, the Global and All Inclusive Agreement, and the Pretoria Agreements.

The Lusaka Agreement had four provisions: commencement of the Inter-Congolese Dialogue (ICD), creation of MONUC, disarmament, and creation of a 30 kilometer wide DMZ along the established front lines. Despite the agreement, fighting continued until Laurent Desire Kabila was assassinated in 2001. His son, Joeseph Kabila, assumed the presidency and was more cooperative in moving forward with the Lusaka Agreement. In particular, his government participated in the ICD, which lasted from April 2002-April 2003. The ICD produced results with the signing of the Global and All Inclusive Agreement that provided the broad outlines for the establishment of a transitional government. Until elections could be held, Kabila would maintain the presidency alongside four vice presidents from the various opposition groups. The Global and All Inclusive Agreement was bolstered by two other bilateral agreements in 2002 between the DRC and their primary antagonists—the Pretoria Agreement with Rwanda and the Luanda Agreement with Uganda.

As determined by the Lusaka Agreement, the United Nations Mission in the Democratic Republic of Congo (MONUC) was established in 1999 under the auspices of UNSC resolutions 1279 and 1291. The latter resolution clearly granted MONUC a Chapter VII mandate "to protect civilians under imminent threat of physical violence."[69] Unfortunately for the civilians in the

DRC, this mandate was at the bottom of a long list of other peacekeeping tasks and was not

clearly understood across MONUC military formations. As a result, UNSC resolution 1565 was

adopted in October 2004 which clearly made the protection of civilians the highest priority. The

top two mandates of this resolution were to maintain a presence to discourage violence and to

protect threatened civilians.

In the context of these resolutions, MONUC operated within three distinct phases. Phase

I consisted of the initial deployment of military observers to monitor the implementation of the

Lusaka agreement. When the Pretoria agreements were signed, Phase II began and was focused

on the transition of the DRC from war to national unity according to the General and All

Inclusive Agreement. The mandate outlined in UNSC resolution 1291 governed these two

phases. Phase III began in October 2004 as MONUC began preparation for national and local

elections, and it is also the month in which the UNSC passed resolution 1565 making the

protection of civilians a priority mandate for MONUC. Finally, Phase IV started in 2006 after the

DRC completed elections.[70] This case study is primarily concerned with Phase II and III in

which MONUC confronted a problem with violence against civilians in the eastern provinces.

After the Pretoria agreements were signed and Phase II began, MONUC personnel

considered the situation in the DRC a post-conflict environment.[71] This meant that they were

_____

[69] United Nations, "*MONUC Mandate*,"
http://www.un.org/en/peacekeeping/missions/monuc/mandate.shtml (accessed February 28, 2013).

[70] Denis M. Tull, "Peacekeeping in the Democratic Republic of the Congo: Waging Peace and Fighting War," *International Peacekeeping* 16, no.2 (April): 215–230.

[71] Autesserre, 65–68.

primarily focused on ensuring the implementation of the requirements within the various ceasefire agreements such as elections, the withdrawal of foreign troops, disarmament of rebel forces, and the integration of rebel fighters into the Armed Forces of the Democratic Republic of the Congo (FARDC). The focus on implementing the treaty reflects the legal positivist heuristic the need for a sovereign ruler with whom to interact. From the perspective of MONUC personnel, local conflicts in the Kivu region were, for the most part, the concern of the transitional government. To this end, MONUC military units focused on the protection of military observers and UN facilities/equipment.

The lack of civilian protection allowed the continued massacre of civilians in the Kivu region. MONUC considered outbreaks of violence in eastern provinces instances of postconflict crises and deployed military personnel as necessary to restore order after raping, kidnapping, and murder already occurred. Despite the fact that UNSC resolutions 1291 clearly authorized MONUC to conduct operations to protect civilians, there was confusion within MONUC on operational approaches. For example, the Nepalese and Pakistani battalions conducted offensive operations against the perpetrators, but the Indian battalions forbade its troops from engaging in offensive actions.[72] The situation deteriorated to the point that the EU dispatched a mostly French force in 2003 to the Ituri district of Bunia province to prevent mass atrocities. Known as Operation Artemis, the three month mission had some success in restoring basic order. However, fueled by spoilers to the peace process, local tensions in the Kivu region reignited after the end of Operation Artemis.

Laurent Nkunda was a rebel leader within the RCD-G, and he refused to integrate into the Armed Forces of the Democratic Republic of Congo (FARDC).[73] Instead, he continued to lead

---

[72] Ibid., 225.

attacks against civilians in an effort to spoil the peace process. In May 2004, Nkunda advanced on Bikuva, which is the capital city of South Kivu. Although UN personnel and FARDC were present and had access to attack helicopters, they chose not to defend the town. FARDC forces simply retreated from the area and MONUC military personnel withdrew to their compound. Civilians were left to face the wrath of Nkunda's undisciplined rebel group. The attack resulted in the death of 88 civilians and 25,000 internally displaced persons.[74] Having lost faith in MONUC's ability and will to protect them, the civilians in the Kivu region began protesting against the mission. This public backlash resulted in UN security resolution 1565.

The passage of UNSC resolution 1565 reemphasized the civilian protection aspect of UNSC 1291 and marked the beginning of Phase III of MONUC's operations in the DRC. The resolution was passed because MONUC realized that violence in the Kivus could destabilize the national level political progress. In the execution of this renewed mandate, MONUC deployed more forces to the east under the command of General Patrick Cammaert who conducted several effective offensive operations in pursuit of the perpetrators. However, these operations resulted in unintended civilian casualties and an increase in reprisal attacks against civilians. In response, the Department of Peacekeeping Operations (DPKO) at the UN forbade further offensive operations. This allowed rebel groups needed space to resume their attacks against civilians.

MONUC had mixed success in the DRC. On one hand, they successfully managed the end of the Second Congo War with the withdrawal of foreign troops and the establishment of the transitional government. These successes led to a decrease in the overall level of violence. However, a singular focus on national level issues caused MONUC to overlook the instability in

---

[73] Julie Reynaert, *MONUC/MONUSCO and Civilian Protection in the Kivus*, International Peace Information Service, http://www.ipisresearch.be/publications_detail.php?id=327 (Date accessed: February 23, 2013).

[74] Reynaert, 16.

the Kivu region where violence continued unabated. The result was one of the bloodiest genocides on the African continent.[75] In terms of preventing mass atrocities, the MONUC mission was a failure. Between 2001-2007, "the estimate of war-related deaths stood at about 3.5 million; in 2007 it had reached more than 5 million."[76] Although there was a glimmer of hope to change some of this reality with the Cammeraet offensives in 2004, the opportunity quickly passed when the DPKO ordered a cessation of operations.

Liberia: Low Level Intervention

The 1990 deployment of ECOMOG to end the Liberian civil war was the first intervention that ECOWAS ever attempted. As a result, there was much debate among the member states about what procedural mechanism legitimized intervention in the internal affairs of a member country. Once the decision was made, ECOMOG deployed a peace keeping force of 3,000 soldiers.[77] However, due to the resistance from rebel forces inside Liberia, ECOMOG changed its mission from peace keeping to peace enforcement.

Liberia is an ethnically diverse country. The four dominant tribes are the Gio, Mano, Mandigo, and Krahn. Liberia is often considered America's unofficial colony due to the fact that many former slaves from the United States were repatriated to the country in the middle of the Nineteenth Century. These repatriated slaves took on an identity known as Americo-Liberian and constitute less than three percent of the population; however, this group held much political

---

[75]Herbert F. Weiss, *Responsibility to Protect: The Global Moral Compact for the 21st Century,* edited by Richard H. Cooper and Juliette Voinov Kohler (New York: Palgrave Macmillan, 2009), 116–128.

[76] Ibid., 123.

[77] Comfort Ero, "ECOWAS and the Subregional Peacekeeping in Liberia," *The Journal of Humanitarian Assistance*: http://sites.tufts.edu/jha/archives/66, accessed (February 10, 2013).

power during most of the modern history of the country. The political dominance of the Americo-Liberian group increased the animosity of the indigenous population and created the conditions for civil war.

In 1980, Master Sergeant Samuel Doe, a Krahn by ethnicity, led a successful military coup against President William Tolbert who was an Americo-Liberian. Although Doe promised to reform the politics of Liberia by liberating the indigenous of the country, he instead empowered himself and oppressed his countrymen. The Gio and other ethnic groups in the country felt as if the Americo-Liberian tyranny was replaced with a new Krahn tyranny; therefore, Thomas Quiwomkpa led an unsuccessful Gio dominated coup against the Doe regime in late 1985. In response to the failed attempt, Doe unleashed the Krahn dominated Armed Forces of Liberia (AFL) to execute a brutal campaign against Quiwompka's hometown in Nimba County. The Gio responded to this oppression with rebellion.

Charles Taylor (Americo-Liberian) and "Prince" Yormie Johnson (Gio) formed the National Patriotic Front of Liberia (NPFL) to confront the Doe regime. On Christmas Day 1989, they began an offensive operation that "degenerated into ethnic carnage."[78] With the backing of Burkina Faso, Cote D' Ivoire, and Libya, the NPFL achieved success against Doe's AFL despite the fact that Johnson split from Taylor forming the Independent National Patriotic Front of Liberia (INPFL)[79] Regardless of this setback, the NPFL controlled 90 percent of the country and forced Doe to retreat to his presidential office in Monrovia. Doe appealed to ECOWAS for help, but there was some debate as to whether this organization had the procedural legitimacy to intervene.

---

[78] Ero, under "The NPFL Invasion."

[79] Ibid., under "The Decision to Intervene and Sub-regional Politics."

Through prompting from Nigeria and Togo, ECOWAS was established 1975. Its primary purpose was to promote the economic well-being of the countries of West Africa. However, the members of ECOWAS understood that peace and security was fundamental to economic prosperity. Thus, ECOWAS members signed the 1978 Protocol on Non-Aggression at the Third Conference of Heads of State and Government. This protocol followed the UN Article 2(4) norm prohibiting the use of force except in self-defense. Furthermore, member states agreed not to support the internal insurrections of each other. In this way, ECOWAS members hoped to ensure conditions of peace and security among members.

In order to deal with threats from outside the community, ECOWAS developed the Protocol on Mutual Assistance and Defense. According to the terms of this agreement, ECOWAS members agreed to come to the aid of fellow member states in the event of foreign intervention from outside the community. Furthermore, if foreign powers outside the community were supporting subversion within a member state, Article 9 of the protocol stated that head of ECOWAS had the ability to create an intervention force to reestablish peace and security.

Citing the Protocol on Mutual Assistance and Defense, the Standing Mediating Committee of ECOWAS decided to intervene in the Liberian Civil War. They stated three reasons for the decision to intervene: 1-probable regional instability from a refugee crisis, 2-humanitarian concerns and the need to stop the senseless killing of innocent civilians, and 3-Doe requested assistance under the terms of the protocol. Despite these reasons, there were ulterior motives behind the support for intervention, and these motives caused much division of effort. The division fell along the lines of Anglophone and Francophone interstate rivalry.

Although not stated publicly, Francophone members such as Burkina Faso and Cote d'Ivoire wanted to intervene on behalf of Taylor. On the other hand, Anglophone countries such as Nigeria wanted to intervene on behalf of Doe. Given that it supplied 70% of troops to ECOMOG, it is not surprising that Nigeria dominated the intervention.[80] Despite these internal divisions, ECOWAS issued a statement calling for a cessation of hostilities, the establishment of ECOMOG, the establishment of an interim government, elections within 12 months, exclusion of leaders of warring factions from government, and the creation of an emergency fund to support ECOMOG operations. Since he controlled most of the country, Taylor considered the ECOWAS demands ridiculous, and he promised to treat ECOMOG forces as invaders. When they landed in Monrovia in August 1990, Taylor was true to his word.

Although supported by the INFPL and the AFL, the ECOMOG intervention was contested by the NFPL from the very beginning. ECOMOG leaders sided with INFPL and AFL because Taylor's formidable NFPL conducted an artillery offensive from the first moment that the interveners landed on the beach. Thus, the operation soon changed from peace keeping to peace enforcement with ECOMOG confronting the NFPL as an enemy.[81] ECOMOG conducted a strategy of limited offensive against the NFPL. During these initial engagements, Doe was captured, tortured and murdered by INFPL forces.

In the end, ECOMOG succeeded in driving out NFPL forces from Monrovia, and they put in place an interim government. As a result of negotiations, a peace deal was reached between all of the warring factions, and Charles Taylor was elected president in 1995. During his presidency, Taylor pursued selfish interests through an illicit diamond trade with the Revolutionary United Front (RUF) operating in Sierra Leone. As a consequence of his corrupt regime, civil war once again erupted in the country in the late 1990s. He was ousted from power

---

[80] Ibid., under "The Decision to Intervene and Sub-regional Politics."

[81] Rasheed Draman and David Carment, "Managing Chaos in the West African Sub-Region: Assessing the Role of ECOMOG in Liberia," *Journal of Military and Strategic Studies* 6, no. 2 (Fall) http://www.jmss.org/jmss/index.php/jmss/article/view/227, 15–20.

in 2003. In 2010, Taylor was convicted of war crimes and crimes against humanity. He was sentenced to 50 years in prison.

The 1990-91 ECOMOG intervention in Liberia had mixed results. According to Dramen and Carment, "ECOMOG's offensive in Liberia succeeded in containing the conflict, at least for a short period, preventing the situation from degenerating into genocidal proportions like the type of all out slaughter witnessed between April and July 1994 in Rwanda."[82] However, Ero points out that ECOMOG was so focused on offensive operations that they practiced "indiscriminate attacks on civilians."[83] Furthermore, the June 1993 massacre of 600 Liberians at a Harbel refugee camp presents an example of a failure to protect. According to a UN investigation of the incident, AFL troops were responsible for the massacre, but ECOMOG, upon learning of the incident, "treated the matter as if it were not its direct responsibility."[84] In short, ECOMOG did achieve short term success in preventing large scale genocide, but a lack of commitment to first principles of increasing the common good of the community diminishes the efficacy of the humanitarian aspect of the mission.

Sierra Leone

The British intervention in Sierra Leone in 2000 is a case study in which a minimum level intervention achieved a high level of efficacy. However, in analyzing this case, two important variables need to be considered. First, the British deployment followed a 1998 ECOMOG low level intervention. This low level intervention evolved to a high level

---

[82] Dramen and Carment, 17.

[83] Ero under "ECOWAS and ECOMOG Intervention in Liberia."

[84] Ibid.

intervention with the deployment of the United Nations Mission in Sierra Leone (UNAMSIL). Second, although the British intervention was unilateral, Secretary General Koffi Annan gave tacit approval to the British unilateral actions. However, once British troops were in Sierra Leone, he requested that British forces fall under the high level intervention being conducted by ECOMOG and UNAMSIL. The British government refused such offers which made their intervention unilateral and, more important to this study, outside the bounds of a formal UNSC resolution. In assessing the efficacy of the British operation, it is important to keep these relevant variables in mind.

Sierra Leone is a former British colony and tribal society. The two largest tribes are the Temne and Mende.[85] Freetown has a large population of Creoles who trace their history back to freed Jamaican slaves repopulated to Africa by the British in the eighteenth century. Sierra Leone's economy is dependent on agriculture and the export of raw materials. In particular, the export of diamonds is a source of lucrative revenue.

After Sierra Leone achieved independence in 1961, the Mende dominated All People's Congress (APC), led by Siaka Stevens, won a close election. During that time, he declared a state of emergency and increasingly consolidated power through intimidation, manipulation, and political executions. The Temne dominated Sierra Leone People's Party (SLPP) resisted Stevens' rule, but he built up an effective and brutal security apparatus that squashed attempts to effect change. When he left office in 1985, Stevens appointed Joseph Saidu Momoh as his replacement; Momoh continued the government's corrupt and repressive policies. His assumption of power served as the catalyst for the establishment of the Revolutionary United Front (RUF).

The RUF was founded in 1991 by Foday Sankoh who was a Temne tribesman and fierce

---

[85] Andrew Dorman, *Blair's Successful War: British Military Intervention in Sierra Leone* (London: Ashgate, 2009), 29–32.

opponent of the APC. In its formative stages, the RUF received popular support as an organization promising political reform and fair treatment for all tribes. However, their tactics revealed them as nothing more than a criminal gang bent on the exploitation of the Sierra Leonean people. They rejected traditional guerilla warfare tactics choosing instead to advance their cause through forced conscription of children and sexual enslavement of girls. To discourage resistance, RUF fighters hacked off limbs of civilians for propaganda effect.[86]

Central to the problem was the battle for the diamond wealth of the country. Charles Taylor, president of the neighboring country of Liberia, provided the RUF with financial backing through an illicit diamond trade. RUF units captured diamond fields from the Sierra Leone government and smuggled the gems into neighboring Liberia where they were passed to Taylor in exchange for weapons and money. In this way, it seems that the RUF was primarily a criminal organization with politics as a secondary and distant concern.

As a result of his inability to deal with RUF, Momoh was ousted in a 1992 coup. Valentine Strasser took control of Sierra Leone under the auspices of the National Provisional Ruling Council (NPRC). However, the NPRC was just as ineffective in defeating the RUF. By 1995, the RUF had captured three of Sierra Leon's largest diamond fields thus depriving the NPRC of its primary source of revenue. The SLA was in complete shambles and unable to conduct an effective defense of the capital. Faced with this situation, Strasser turned to Executive Outcomes, a private military contracting company to fight the RUF.[87]

EO mobilized a small militia group known as the Komojas and what was left of the SLA to push back the RUF and recapture the lost diamond fields. Due to these successful operations,

---

[86] Ibid., 45–50.

[87] Ibid., 57–60.

Sierra Leone achieved enough political space to conduct a presidential election in 1996. These elections resulted in Ahmad Kabbah's election to the presidency. After the NPRC handed power to Kabbah, he began negotiations with RUF leaders. The result was the Abijan Peace Agreement. This agreement promised peace in exchange for a general amnesty extension to RUF fighters and the expulsion of EO within five weeks of signing the treaty. The signing of this treaty resulted in a brief period of tense peace in the country. However, in early 1997, Major Johnny Koroma, a low level SLA officer, executed a coup against the Kabbah government because he was disgruntled with the fact that Kabbah worked with the Komojas militia. Kabbah went into exile in Guinea, and Koroma made an alliance with the RUF.

In response to the perceived undercutting of democracy in Sierra Leone, ECOMOG deployed to Sierra Leone to conduct a low level intervention in 1997. The objective of the intervention was to oust the Koroma regime. Koroma and the RUF defeated this intervention and pushed ECOMOG out of Freetown. The RUF celebrated their victory by looting, raping, and murdering many Creole citizens. In early 1998, ECOMOG tried again to oust the Koroma regime with a more robust force. In this renewed operation, they were successful. The UNSC capitalized on this success with the passing of resolution 1181, which established the United Nations Observation Mission in Sierra Leone (UNOMSIL). Comprised of 70 observers and a small support contingency, UNOMSIL was to monitor conditions on the ground between the warring factions.[88] In December 1998, the RUF launched a counteroffensive against ECOMOG. ECOMOG forces again withdrew from Freetown, and UNOMSIL personnel were evacuated to Guinea. When RUF forces entered Freetown in early 1999, they once again committed mass atrocities against the Creole population.

---

[88] Ibid., 55–60.

41

Being preoccupied with events in Kosovo, British diplomats pressured Kabbah into negotiating with RUF leaders in an effort to end the fighting. The result was the July 1999 Lome Peace Agreement in which the government of Sierra Leone recognized the RUF as a legitimate political party. The agreement required the phased withdrawal of ECOMOG forces, the reestablishment of an integrated SLA, and the guaranteed safety of UNOMSIL military observers. It also authorized a neutral peacekeeping force comprised of UNOMSIL and ECOMOG to disarm, demobilize, and reintegrate (DDR) all combatants of the RUF, Kojoma militias, and Sierra Leone Army. In order to fulfill this final requirement, UNSC resolution 1270 established the United Nations Mission in Sierra Leone (UNAMSIL).

UNAMSIL was a more significant force than UNAMSOL. It was authorized a force of 6,000 personnel to implement UNSC resolution 1270's DDR mandate. Furthermore, the resolution authorized UNAMSIL forces to exercise Chapter VII authority to "take the necessary action to ensure the security and freedom of movement of its personnel and, within its capabilities and areas of deployment, to afford protection to civilians under imminent threat of physical violence."[89] However, despite this authorization, the commander of UNAMSIL, Brigadier Vijay Jetley, effectively operated under a Chapter VI mandate whereby DDR functions were executed only if all parties agreed.

Despite these difficulties, UNAMSIL began its efforts to implement the DDR requirements. One of the tenets of the agreement was that DDR camps would be established in RUF territory no later than September of 2000. To this end, UNAMSIL established its first DDR camps in RUF territory in April 2000. Ten RUF fighters immediately reported to the camp to begin the DDR process. Local RUF commanders were furious that UNAMSIL had accepted the

---

[89] United Nations Security Council, Resolution 1973, (New York, 2000), http://daccess-dds-ny.un.org/doc/UNDOC/GEN/N99/315/02/PDF/N9931502.pdf?OpenElement (accessed March 1, 2013).

fighters without consultation. This started a RUF offensive that pushed UNAMSIL forces back to Freetown while kidnapping military observers and entire battalions of UNAMSIL units. Concerned about British civilians in Freetown, Blair authorized his administration to plan a Non-combatant Evacuation (NEO), but his commitment to substantive principles eventually led to an expansion of the mission.

In an April 1999 speech in Chicago, Tony Blair communicated his "doctrine of the international community":

> Now our actions are guided by a more subtle blend of mutual self interest and moral purpose in defending the values we cherish. In the end, values and interests merge. If we can establish and spread the values of liberty, the rule of law, human rights and an open society then that is in our national interests too. The spread of our values makes us safer.[90]

He went on to say, "The most pressing foreign policy problem we face is to identify the circumstances in which we should get actively involved in other people's conflicts."[91] Blair's call for a moral foundation to foreign policy suggests that substantive principles were a key component of his decision-making process vis-à-vis international politics. As this case study demonstrates, these principles guided his decisions in an intervention that evolved from a NEO to a humanitarian intervention to defeat the RUF.[92]

In May 2000, the RUF offensive reached the outskirts of Freetown. As a result, the British government began to plan for the evacuation of Entitled Personnel: British nationals, EU/American nationals, and others based on space available. Dubbed Operation Palliser, there was no disagreement in the government about the need for the evacuation; however, there was

---

[90] Tony Blair, *The Blair Doctrine* (speech, Chicago Business Club, April 22, 1999).

[91] Ibid.

[92] Dorman, 13–28.

disagreement about the extent of the operation. If the British focused merely on evacuating entitled personnel, both UNAMSIL and the Sierra Leone government would be perceived as ineffective and thereby discredited. However, military operations beyond an evacuation to bolster support to these regimes were unpopular with the British public. The dilemma manifested itself in the British governmental departments. Foreign Minister Robin Cook felt the priority should be on maintaining the credibility of UNAMSIL, and Defense Secretary Geoffrey Hoon viewed the evacuation of entitled personnel as the highest priority.[93]

Despite the lack of policy consensus, Brigadier David Richards deployed with an Operational Reconnaissance and Liaison Team to gather intelligence for the impending NEO. After assessing conditions on the ground, Richards authorized 1st Battalion of the Parachute Infantry Regiment (1st Para) and the Amphibious Ready Group (ARG) to seize the airport and conduct a NEO. Within 48 hours, 450 entitled people were evacuated from Sierra Leone.

Events were changing so rapidly that the British government gave Richards and the British High Commissioner full authority to make decisions on the ground. In a meeting at President Kabbah's house, Richards saw a helicopter prepositioned nearby in case Kabbah needed to evacuate the country. Richards informed the president that he would not need to use the helicopter. He made a commitment to President Kabbah that the UK would assist the government it its defense against RUF forces. This was prior to any formal commitment from the Ministry of Defense or the Foreign and Commonwealth Office who were trying to determine what to do next.[94]

Fortunately for Richards, Tony Blair was willing to expand the mission. He agreed with

---

[93] Ibid., 13–28.

[94] David Richards, interview by Allan Little, BBC, May 15, 2002, http://www.youtube.com/watch?v=Dp7Q018O6s4 (accessed November 6, 2012).

Robin Cook that a RUF victory would be a humanitarian and political disaster. In a recent BBC interview, Blair reflected back on the decision saying, "Once we realized that we really could buy a targeted intervention with a limited number of troops who were prepared to stand up and fight if necessary, that we could in fact knock this gangster group out and restore the government. Well, why not?"[95] In this statement, Blair made no reference to procedural approval of the operation. He merely appealed to principles of substantive legitimacy to justify intervention. He made the decision because it was the right thing to do.

As a result of Richards and Blair's decisions, the NEO was followed by a government policy to hold the airport and Freetown until UNAMSIL reinforcements could arrive. To secure this objective, the British identified five tasks: 1-secure the terrain around airport and the outer suburbs of Freetown, 2-relieve UNAMSIL forces besieged in DDR camps in areas north of Freetown, 3-form an alliance with militia groups such as the Kamojos, 4-execute a robust ISR plan to find out the location and capabilities of the RUF, and 5-conduct information operations to communicate British commitment to Sierra Leone.[96] In short, Richards and his officers were operating in a complex adaptive environment, assessing the situation, and reformulating their operational objectives as necessary. Richards' planners expected these tasks to be completed in about a month.

By the end of May, British policy finally caught up with events on the ground, and the result was a longer term commitment to "establish a sustainable peace and security, stable democratic government, the reduction of poverty, respect for human rights and the establishment

---

[95] Tony Blair, interview by Allan Little, BBC, May 15, 2002, http://www.youtube.com/watch?v=Dp7Q018O6s4 (accessed November 6, 2012).

[96] Dorman, 92–94.

of accountable armed forces."[97]   In order to achieve these objectives, the British created Short Term Training Teams (STTT) to retrain what was left of the SLA. Because of this training, the SLA continued to increase its capabilities. With their British advisers, they pushed the RUF out of the diamond fields and rescued captured UN and British hostages. With this kind of long term commitment from Britain, the RUF leaders knew they could no longer survive as a military organization, and they opened to peace negotiations. In November, RUF leaders signed a ceasefire agreement. Although the RUF tried, as was their custom, to renege on the treaty in 2001, they failed because the international community was united in defending Sierra Leone. Diamond embargoes were placed on Liberia thereby cutting the RUF's main source of financial backing. In short, they were defeated.

By every measure, the British operation in Sierra Leone was a success. The NEO evacuation was executed near flawlessly, and the Creole population in Freetown was saved from a replaying of the 1997 and 1999 humanitarian crises. Furthermore, the Sierra Leone government remained a democratic state. Britain has maintained its support to the present. To be sure, this was a much longer commitment than the government anticipated. However, the success of the operation demonstrates that, given the right circumstances, military interventions can work to protect vulnerable populations from abuse.

Libya

Operation Unified Protector, the 2011 NATO led R2P operation in Libya, provides a case study of a maximum level intervention that was successful. This case study is included in order to introduce variation on the dependent variable. The purpose of the operation was to protect civilians from indiscriminate attack from Muammar Qaddafi's military forces. Although debated

---

[97] Ibid., 96

to some extent, this operation is considered a model for future R2P operations.

Muammar Qadaffi came to power in September 1969 when he overthrew King Idris in a bloodless coup. As a disciple of Gabel Nasser, Qadaffi was a proponent of socialist pan-Arabism. In his *Green Book*, he outlined a political philosophy of "rule of the masses," but the masses had little to say in the direction of the country. The 6 million inhabitants of the country benefitted only marginally from Libya's vast oil reserves.[98] GDP per capita in 2010 was estimated to be around $15,000, which is not destitute by international standards.[99] However, considering Libya's oil wealth, there should have been broader prosperity. Qadaffi's mismanagement of the country was the prime reason for the disparity.

In the 1980s, Qadaffi banned all private enterprise in the country and censured speech he felt threatened his regime.[100] The only significant jobs available were those associated with the government. Estimates are that unemployment was 30 percent. Qadaffi's support for terrorist regimes with anti-Western sentiments did not help the country progress out of economic stagnation. The most egregious example of Libyan support of terrorism was the bombing of Pan Am Flight 103 over Lockerbie, Scotland. Actions such as these made Libya an international pariah and diminished enthusiasm for foreign investment in the country.

After the 9/11 terrorist attacks, Qadaffi seemed to soften his stance vis-à-vis the international community. Although he denied association for many years, he finally took responsibility for the Lockerbie bombing. Furthermore, the Qadaffi regime stopped pursuing its

---

[98] Tarik Kafala, "Gaddafi's Quixotic Rule," *BBC*, http://www.bbc.co.uk/news/world-africa-12532929 (accessed March 2, 2011).

[99] CIA World Factbook, "Libya," https://www.cia.gov/library/publications/the-world-factbook/geos/ly.html (accessed March 2, 2011).

[100] Kafala.

nuclear, chemical, and biological weapons programs. These steps were taken to improve Libya's economy, but it turned out to be too late.

In 2011, the Libyan population was caught up in the euphoria of the so called "Arab Spring." The first protests erupted in the western city of Benghazi, a city that Qadaffi distrusted from the beginning of his rule. Eventually, the protests reached the city of Tripoli and turned into a full blown armed rebellion. In response, Qadaffi unleashed the entire arsenal of his military against the rebels. Close air attacks and heavy artillery bombed cities indiscriminately, which caused the deaths of non-combatants. The international community was disturbed by the wanton taking of innocent life, and actions were soon authorized to enforce a no-fly zone to protect the population of Libya. [101]

UNSC resolution 1970 was the first censure of Qadaffi's operations against civilians. In this resolution, the UNSC demanded that Qadaffi end violence and respect the demands of the population.[102] It further urged that the Libyan government respect human rights, ensure safety of foreign nationals, and allow safe passage of medical assistance. After allegations that Qadaffi's forces were attacking protestors, the Arab League requested UN approval for a no fly zone over certain areas of the country.[103] In March 2012, UNSC resolution 1973 was passed authorizing the no-fly zone and calling on member nations to take all necessary measures "to protect civilians

---

[101] Jayshe Bajoria, "Libya and the Responsibility to Protect," *Council on Foreign Relations*, http://www.cfr.org/libya/libya-responsibility-protect/p24480 (accessed February 20, 2013).

[102] United Nations Security Council, *Resolution 1970* (New York, 2011), http://www.un.org/ga/search/view_doc.asp?symbol=S/RES/1970%282011%29 (accessed March 9, 2013).

[103] Albert Bright, "Arab League Approves No Fly Zone. But is it too Late?," *Christian Science Monitor*, http://www.csmonitor.com/World/terrorism-security/2011/0313/Arab-League-approves-no-fly-zone-in-Libya.-But-is-it-too-late (accessed November 30, 2012).

and civilian populated areas under attack in the Libyan Arab Jamahiriya, including Benghazi, while excluding a foreign occupation force of any form on any part of Libyan territory."[104] The exclusion of ground forces left only naval and air means available for the international community. NATO volunteered to take on the challenge.

Operation Unified Protector was a coordinated NATO effort to suppress Qadaffi's ability to target civilian areas. To this end, NATO air and naval forces conducted reconnaissance and surveillance operations to identify threats to civilians. According to official documents, NATO achieved a good bit of success in their efforts to thwart Qadaffi's war making capabilities:

> As of 25 September 2011, NATO and partner aircraft conducted over 24,200 sorties, including over 9,000 strike sorties. NATO actions have destroyed over 5,900 military targets including over 400 artillery or rocket launchers and over 600 tanks or armored vehicles. NATO has also struck over 400 military command and control centers to halt the Qadhafi regime's ability to give orders to its forces. Targeting is done with extreme care and precision, using the weapon with the smallest yield possible, to avoid harm to the Libyan people and their infrastructure.[105]

As these figures suggest, NATO was acting on a broad interpretation of their mandate to protect civilians.

Although UNSC resolution 1973 did not call for regime change, the robust actions of NATO seemed to indicate this was the goal. A March 2011 phone conversation between President Obama and President Erdogan of Turkey in which regime change was discussed seemed to verify that the policy of protecting civilians expanded to the removal of Qadaffi. Despite this phone conversation, officials from the Obama administration denied that regime

---

[104] United Nations Security Council, Resolution 1973 (New York, 2011), http://www.un.org/ga/search/view_doc.asp?symbol=S/RES/1973%282011%29.

[105] NATO Factsheet, http://www.nato.int/cps/en/natolive/71679.htm, (accessed March 10, 2013).

change was the strategic aim in Libya. The purpose of the operation was to protect civilians. However, administration officials qualified this statement with the claim that Qadaffi was no longer fit to rule.[106] Whether or not regime change was the goal in Libya, the reality is that NATO operations were the direct cause for the ouster of Qadaffi. By August 2011, rebel forces were in control of Tripoli. On October 17, Qadaffi, his sons, and approximately 66 others were captured in his hometown of Shirte and subsequently murdered.[107]

Critics of the Libyan intervention point to the massacre in Shirte as evidence of the failure of the intervention to protect humanitarian interests in Libya. While this was indeed a stain on the operation, defenders of the intervention argue that observers must consider a counterfactual. If there was no intervention, the killing would have been worse than that which resulted in Shirte. David Clark examined the response to other Arab revolts to support this claim:

> In the past, Arab dictators who have suppressed uprisings tended not to show a great deal of mercy after the fact. When a rebellion in the Syrian town Hama was put down in 1982, the president's brother boasted of killing 38,000. It is thought that as many as 100,000 died following the 1991 Shia uprising in Iraq. In Libya itself, a mass grave was recently uncovered containing the bodies of 1,200 victims of the 1996 Abu Salim prison massacre.[108]

Therefore, in terms of protecting, the Libyan operation seems to have achieved some success.[109]

---

[106] Sam Youngman and Jordan Fabian, "White House Denies Regime Change is Part of Libyan Mission," *The Hill,* http://thehill.com/homenews/campaign/151191-white-house-suggests-regime-change-is-goal-of-libya-mission (accessed March 5, 2013).

[107] Reuters, *Many Libyans Executed in Qadaffi Capture: Report,* http://www.reuters.com/article/2012/10/17/us-libya-gaddafi-report-idUSBRE89G06820121017 (accessed March 3, 2013).

[108] David Clark, Libyan Intervention a Success Despite Aftermath's Atrocities," *Guardian,* October 28, http://www.guardian.co.uk/commentisfree/2011/oct/28/intervention-libya-success (accessed March 8, 2013).

[109] Ramesh Thakur, "UN Breathes Life into Responsibility to Protect," *The Star* http://www.thestar.com/opinion/editorialopinion/article/957664--un-breathes-life-into-responsibility-to-protect (accessed November 23, 2012).

The civil war stopped, and the government is in the process of implementing democratic reforms.

CONCLUSION

There are many causal variables that relate to efficacy in R2P operations (e.g., economics, institutional capacity, and quality of intervening force) . This monograph does not claim that legitimacy is a necessary and sufficient causal variable; however, the case studies presented suggest that interpretations of legitimacy do have limited explanatory power in the efficacy of R2P operations. Based on these case studies, it seems that a legal positivist heuristic decreases their efficacy. The efficacy seems to decrease as the level of legitimacy increases from minimum to maximum level interventions. In this way, extended efforts to link R2P operations to procedural expressions of sovereign will causes three problems: mandate conflict, macro-level organizational culture, and institutional manipulability.

One might think the first problem could be solved with more clearly written documents, but the case studies demonstrate that this is not the solution. In the DRC, there was a clearly articulated mandate to protect civilians, but MONUC, a high level intervention force, refused to address the violence in the Kivus region. Failures such as these are causally related to the international community's conflicting heuristic when interpreting mandate requirements. For example, some battalions of MONUC conducted offensive operations to protect civilians (Nepal) while others remained neutral (India).[110] In the former case, the battalion commander seems to have appealed to a heuristic of first principles in the responsibility to protect people under Chapter VII authority. The latter commander chose to adhere to a legal positivist heuristic of a peacekeeping force operating under a Chapter VI mandate thereby remaining neutral in an

---

[110] Autesserre, 225.

attempt to obtain a peaceful settlement. As Krain points out in his research, a neutrality heuristic tends to lead to failure in R2P operations.[111]

As the level of legitimacy decreases, heuristic assumptions seem to align more easily, which increases operational speed and flexibility. For example, ECOMOG's low level intervention against Charles Taylor in Liberia changed rapidly from peace keeping to peace enforcement, and the British minimum level intervention in Sierra Leone changed from a NEO to a long term state building commitment. As a result, ECOMOG probably prevented genocide in Monrovia, and the UK most certainly prevented a massacre in Freetown. However, ECOMOG's use of force that resulted in civilian casualties suggests there are limits to the power of substantive legitimacy. In the end, outcome legitimacy as it relates to the first principle of doing no harm to non-combatants is the most important factor in efficacious operations.

Severine Autesserre suggests there is a tendency for participants in maximum and high level interventions to focus too much on macro-level issues.[112] This macro-level focus tends to make intervention forces blind to lower level violence. In the DRC, MONUC was completely focused on legal positivist issues such as elections to establish a sovereign and the implementation of peace treaties among the various states in the region. As a result, MONUC underestimated local violence in the Kivus. A macro-level focus decreased efficacy in the Sudan as well. International leaders placed too much confidence in the mitigating effect of legal positivist instruments such as the HFCA and the Joint Communiqué, each a written expression of sovereign will. Overreliance on such instruments renders the international community unresponsive to first principles as demonstrated when the COI determined the violence in Darfur something short of genocide.

---

[111] Matthew Krain, "International Intervention and the Severity of Genocides and Politicides," *International Studies Quarterly* 49, (September 2005): 363–387.

[112] Autesserre, 248–262.

Finally, the legal positivist heuristic enables unscrupulous characters to manipulate international institutions. For example, Bashir was able to manipulate the character of the UNAMID intervention force, and the ECOMOG intervention was hampered by the internal politics between Anglophile and Francophile contingents. These machinations are often overlooked by other members of international organizations because politics and national interest are the prerogative of sovereign leaders. However, as Gareth Evans asserts, the successful implementation of the R2P principle requires that the international community look at problems from the perspective of the victims, not the sovereigns. Unfortunately, obtaining this perspective is difficult in an international political system dominated by a legal positivist heuristic.

BIBLIOGRAPHY

Abbot, H. Porter. *The Cambridge Introduction to Narrative*. Cambridge: Cambridge University Press, 2008.

Annan, Koffi. "1999 Speech to the General Assembly." Secretary-General address to the UN General Assembly, New York, NY, September 20, 1999.

Autesserre, Severine. *The Trouble with the Congo: Local Violence and the Failure of Peacebuilding*. Cambridge: Cambridge University Press, 2010.

Badescu, Cristina and Linnea Bergholm. "The African Union." In *The International Politics of Mass Atrocities: The Case of Darfur*, edited by David R. Black and Paul D. Williams. New York: Routledge Publishers, 2010.

Bajoria, Jayshe. "Libya and the Responsibility to Protect." *Council on Foreign Relations*, http://www.cfr.org/libya/libya-responsibility-protect/p24480, (accessed November 8, 2012).

Bellamy, Alex J. *Responsibility to Protect*. Cambridge: Polity Press, 2009.

Berman, Nathaniel. "Intervention in a 'Divided World': Axes of Legitimacy." *The European Journal of International Law* 17, no. 4 (2006): 743–769.

Bjola, Corneliu. "Legitimacy and the Use of Force: Bridging the Analytical—Normative Divide." *Review of International Studies* 34 (October 2008): 627–644.

Blair, Tony. *The Blair Doctrine*, Prime Minister's Speech to the Chicago Business Club, April 22, 1999. http://www.pbs.org/newshour/bb/international/jan-june99/blair_doctrine4-23.html (accessed January 15, 2013).

Blair, Tony. Interview by Allan Little for BBC, May 15, 2002. http://www.youtube.com/watch?v=Dp7Q018O6s4. (accessed January 12, 2013).

Bright, Albert. "Arab League Approves No Fly Zone. But is it too Late." *Christian Science Monitor*, http://www.csmonitor.com/World/terrorism-security/2011/0313/Arab-League-approves-no-fly-zone-in-Libya.-But-is-it-too-late. (accessed November 30, 2012).

Bull, Hedley. "Natural Law and International Relations," *British Journal of International Studies* 5, no. 2 (1979): 171–181.

Clark, David. "Libyan Intervention a Success Despite Aftermath's Atrocities." *Guardian*, October 28. http://www.guardian.co.uk/commentisfree/2011/oct/28/intervention-libya-success, (accessed March 8, 2013).

Dorman, Andrew. *Blair's Successful War: British Military Intervention in Sierra Leone*.

London: Ashgate, 2009.

Draman, Rasheed and David Carment. "Managing Chaos in the West African Sub-Region: Assessing the Role of ECOMOG in Liberia." *Journal of Military and Strategic Studies* 6, no. 2 (Fall). http://www.jmss.org/jmss/index.php/jmss/article/view/227, (accessed March 10, 2013), 15–20.

Ero, Comfort. "ECOWAS and the Subregional Peacekeeping in Liberia." *The Journal of Humanitarian Assistance*: http://sites.tufts.edu/jha/archives/66, (accessed February 10, 2013).

Evans, Gareth. "The Responsibility to Protect: From an Idea to an International Norm." in *Responsibility to Protect: The Global Moral Compact for the 21st Century*. Edited by Richard H. Cooper and Juliette Voinov Kohler. New York: Palgrave-Macmillan, 2009.

Evans, Gareth and Mohamed Sahnoun. "The Responsibility to Protect." *Foreign Affairs* 81, no. 6 (Nov/Dec 2002), 99–110.

Evans, Gareth and Mohamed Sahnoun. *Report of the International Convention on Intervention and Sovereignty*, http://responsibilitytoprotect.org/ICISS%20Report.pdf. (accessed, January 12, 2013).

Fabienne, Peter. "Political Legitimacy." *The Stanford Encyclopedia of Philosophy (Summer 2010 Edition)*, ed. Edward N. Zalta. http://plato.stanford.edu/archives/sum2010/entries/legitimacy/ (accessed March 5, 2013).

Genocide Prevention Task Force. *Preventing Genocide: A Blueprint for U.S. Policymakers*. Chaired by Madeleine K. Albright and William S. Cohen. Washington D.C.: United States Institute for Peace, 2008.

Hall, Stephen. "The Persistent Spectre: Natural Law, International Order and the Limits of Legal Positivism." *European Journal of International Law* 12 no. 2 (2001): 269-307.

Hehir, Aidan. *Humanitarian Intervention After Kosovo: Iraq, Darfur and the Record of Global Civil* Society. New York: Palgrave Macmillan, 2008.

Holzgrefe, J.L. Holzgrefe and Robert O. Keohane. *Humanitarian Intervention: Ethical, Legal and Political Dilemmas*. New York: Cambridge University Press, 2003.

Hurrell, Andrew. "Legitimacy and the Use of Force: Can the Circle be Squared." *Review of International Studies* 31(December 2005): 15–32.

International Commission of Inquiry. *Report of the International Commission of Inquiry on Darfur to the United Nations Secretary General*. New York (2004).

Jibril, Abdelbagi A. M. *Past and Future of UNAMID: Tragic Failure or Glorious Success?* Geneva: Darfur Relief and Documentation Center, 2010.

Kafala, Tarik. "Gaddafi's Quixotic Rule." BBC.

http://www.bbc.co.uk/news/world-africa-12532929, (accessed March 2, 2011).

King, Gary, Robert O. Keohane, and Sidney Verba. *Designing Social Inquiry: Scientific Inference in Qualitative Research.* Princeton: Princeton University Press, 1994.

Krain, Matthew. "International Intervention and the Severity of Genocides and Politicides." *International Studies Quarterly* 49, (September 2005): 363–387.

Krasner, Stephen. *Sovereignty: Organized Hypocrisy.* Princeton: Princeton University Press, 1999.

MacIntyre, Alasdair. *After Virtue*, 3rd ed. Notre Dame: Notre Dame University Press, 2008.

NATO Factsheet, http://www.nato.int/cps/en/natolive/71679.htm. (accessed March 10, 2013).

Pattison, James. *Humanitarian Intervention and the Responsibility to Protect: Who Should Intervene.* New York: Oxford University Press, 2010.

Philpott, Daniel. *Revolutions in Sovereignty.* Princeton: Princeton University Press, 2001.

Regan, Patrick M. "Conditions of Successful Third-Party Intervention in Intrastate Conflicts." *The Journal of Conflict Resoluton* 40, no.2 (1996): 336–359.

Reuters, *Many Libyans Executed in Qadaffi Capture: Report*, http://www.reuters.com/article/2012/10/17/us-libya-gaddafi-report-idUSBRE89G06820121017. (accessed March 3, 2013).

Reynaert, Julie, *MONUC/MONUSCO and Civilian Protection in the Kivus*, International Peace Information Service, http://www.ipisresearch.be/publications_detail.php?id=327, (Date accessed: February 23, 2013).

Richards, David, interview by Allan Little, BBC, May 15, 2002, http://www.youtube.com/watch?v=Dp7Q018O6s4. (accessed January 13, 2013).

Sewell, Sarah, Dwight Raymond, and Sally Chin. *Mass Atrocities Response Operations: A Military Planner's Handbook.* Boston: Harvard University Press, 2010.

Thakur, Ramesh. "UN Breathes Life into Responsibility to Protect" *The Star* http://www.thestar.com/opinion/editorialopinion/article/957664--un-breathes-life-into-responsibility-to-protect. (accessed November 23, 2012).

Totten, Samuel. "Saving Lives in Darfur, 2003-2006?" in *The World and Darfur: International Response to Crimes Against Humanity in Western Sudan.* Edited by Amanda F. Gryzyb. Kingston: McGill-Queen's University Press, 2009.

Tull, Denis M. "Peacekeeping in the Democratic Republic of the Congo: Waging Peace and Fighting War" *International Peacekeeping* 16, no.2 (April): 215–230.

United Nations, "MONUC Mandate,"

http://www.un.org/en/peacekeeping/missions/monuc/mandate.shtml. (accessed February 28, 2013).

United Nations Security Council. Resolution 1973. New York, 2011. http://www.un.org/ga/search/view_doc.asp?symbol=S/RES/1973%282011%29. (accessed February 21, 2013).

Weiss, Herbert F. *Responsibility to Protect: The Global Moral Compact for the 21st Century.* Edited by Richard H. Cooper and Juliette Voinov Kohler. New York: Palgrave Macmillan, 2009.

Weiss, Thomas G. "The Sunset of Humanitarian Intervention? The Responsibility to Protect in a Unipolar Era." *Security Dialouge* 35, no. 2 (2004): 135–153.